PRAYERS
FOR LITTLE CHILDREN

1st Prize
Lower Juniors

Presented to

Sarah

July 1980.

Bible Club

Competition

C.L.C. BOOKSHOP, 5 Higham Pl., New

PRAYERS

FOR LITTLE CHILDREN

For fives to eights.

by Elspeth M. Stephenson

Illustrated by Jean Carruthers

ARK PUBLISHING
47 Marylebone Lane, London, W1M 6AX

© Text: Elspeth M. Stephenson 1973
© Illustrations: Scripture Union 1973
First published 1973 in Tell it to Jesus.
This selection published 1980

ISBN 0 86201 006 3

Printed in England by McCorquodale (Newton) Ltd., Newton-le-Willows, Lancashire.

To Heather, Dawn, and Mark

Preface

These prayers may be shared by the whole family, but have been planned to be within the comprehension of children in the five to eight age-group and to appeal particularly to them. Some may be able to read the prayers for themselves, while others will need an adult to read with them.

I believe also that teachers and leaders will find these prayers very useful with infants and younger juniors in day schools, and the same group in the Sunday School and church context. The more personal prayers may easily be changed for corporate use by substituting 'we' for 'I'.

E.M.S.

Contents

God the greatest maker

Great God in heaven,
You are so clever to know everything in the world.
You are so big to have made everything in the world.
You are so kind to want to have each of us for a friend.
Thank you.

God,
   when the rain crashes on the road and jumps up
     again;
   when the thunder cracks and booms up in the clouds;
   when the waves race on to the sandy shore;
We think how big and wonderful you are.
But I'm glad you care about little things as well,
   —about daisies closing their petals at night;
   —about the twinkly spiders' webs after the rain;
   —about the little spotted ladybird.
Thank you.

Dear God,
We see bulldozers crunching up the hard earth;
We hear jet aeroplanes whining across the sky;
We read of ocean liners moving across the water.
Thank you that you made men clever enough to plan and
make these machines. Thank you that you gave them the
coal and the iron and the wood to work with. Help us to
understand that they could do nothing without you.

God, you have given us a lovely world to live in. Thank
you for all the machines that help us. We're glad we have
cars and boats and aeroplanes to travel about in. We're
glad we have the telephone so that we can talk to people
far away. We thank you for the machines in our homes—
for the washing machine; for the fridge and the ....
Thank you so much.

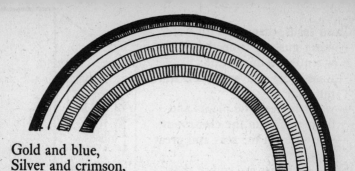

Gold and blue,
Silver and crimson,
Buttercup yellow and white.
Thank you for colours everywhere, God.
When we look at television it's often black and white and grey. I'm glad we don't live in a black and white and grey world. You have made it lovely to look at, with dappled skies and yellow daffodils; with red and green apples and chocolate-brown earth.
Thank you especially for the beautiful rainbow you make
in the sky.

The stars shine like lots of torches hung in the sky.
You put them there.
The spacemen travel millions of miles to the moon.
You put it there.
It's a great big world at night, God.
You made the dark, too, so we needn't be afraid.
It's your world.
And you made us. Thank you.

Thank you, God, that—
You made the cow who gives us
    creamy milk to drink.
You made the sheep with wool for
    making warm clothes.
You made the hens who give us
    eggs for breakfast.
Thank you, God.

Lord Jesus, thank you for water
—water gushing from the tap
  when we're thirsty;
—water deep and warm and fun in
  the bath;
—water to keep the plants and
  flowers alive in the classroom;
—salt water in the seas and great
  oceans.
Some countries are so hot that
  water is very precious.
Thank you that we have plenty
  where I live.

I feel so small, sometimes, God.
The trees in the wood tower above
  me.
The blocks of flats rise high in the
  sky.
Even Mummy and Daddy are so
  much bigger than I am.
Sometimes I feel I'm not
  important at all.
I'm glad you've made little things
  as well as big things, God
—the tiny fish and running ants;
—the specks of sand and hairs on
  my legs.
Thank you that little things are
  special to you as well as big
  things.

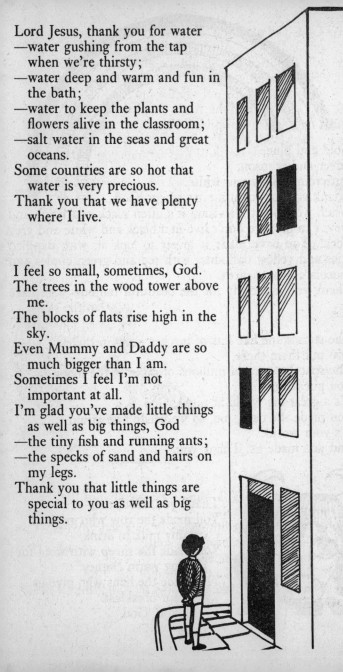

Dear God, I'm glad you've made living creatures.
I've watched a hairy caterpillar loop its way across a leaf;
I've seen a spotted thrush plunge into the bird-bath;
I've heard a cat purring;
I've felt a dog wag his tail against my legs.
One day I looked and there was a bud on the twig, and the
next day a beautiful pink flower had burst out.
Thank you, God, for *life*.
All these creatures couldn't live without you who made
them.
Thank you, too, that I have *life*.
—Life, to stretch my arms towards the sky.
—Life, to hear a clock ticking or an aeroplane whine.
—Life, to blow bubbles through a ring.
I'm really alive, just as you made me.
Thank you, God.

Dear God,
We've tried to make flowers in plasticine, but they're
not as small as yours.
We've tried to paint butterflies in reds and yellows,
but they're not as pretty as yours.
We've made sighing noises,
but they weren't like the sound of the wind.
You are the greatest maker. Thank you, God, for all the
lovely things you've made.

God made me

Seeds are only little dry brown things, but they grow into delicious fruit and beautiful flowers.
Thank you for the *life* you've put in the little brown seeds.
Rabbits and dogs and cats and hens come from tiny specks.
Thank you for the *life* you've put there to grow.
Baby sister (brother) came from a very tiny speck inside her (his) mother.
So did I.
So did every person.
Thank you for the *life* you put in that tiny speck.
You made life.

Tick, tock, tick, tock.
That big clock has a loud tick.
Daddy's watch, if I put my ear to it, has a tiny, whispery tick.
They both show time going by.
Time—for breakfast.
Time—for school.
Time—for bed.
Thank you for moments when time goes quickly, times of fun and good things. Show me that you have given me every minute of time to use as best I can.

My body works in exciting ways.
When I get hungry, then I know it needs some food.
When I get tired, then I know it needs to rest.
Thank you that you've made my body like that.
Thank you, too, for food and sleep. Amen.

.... has a new baby brother (sister*). It's funny to
think that we were once like that. He just sleeps and lies in
a pram and cries and drinks milk. His little finger nails are
perfectly made. One day he'll grow to be a man. Please
help him to love you as he grows to be a boy and then a
man. Keep him safe and happy too.

*If 'sister', watch for other words in this prayer that will need
changing, too.

God cares for me

Dear God, we can't see you, but we know you are there.
We see leaves blowing off trees.
We hear the roaring in the chimneys.
We know the wind does this, though we can't see it.
In the same way, we can't see you but we know you are
   there.

Sometimes I'm driving a fast train, roaring through a
   tunnel.
Sometimes I'm a spaceman soaring up to the moon.
Sometimes I'm the cleverest teacher in the big school.
But I'm just pretending.
I'm not really one of these important people.
Thank you that I'm special to you, God.
Thank you that you love me.

Dear God, I'm glad that you want us to know you and love
you. You're so great and powerful and strong, yet you
don't hide away from us like a king in a castle. You want to
get to know us. You want us to love you. Thank you that
Jesus came to this world to show us what you are like.
Amen.

Father God,
You know all our thoughts each
 moment of the day.
Thank you that you still love us
 with a good father's love.
You know the bad thoughts of
 ours which no one else knows.
Thank you that you still love us
 with a good father's love.
You know the good thoughts of
 ours, even when they don't
 show.
Thank you that you still love us
 with a good father's love.

Dear God, when I'm grown up I
might want to be an engine-driver,
or an air-pilot, or a nurse, or a
teacher, or .... God, you
know all about me now, and you'll
know all about me when I'm grown
up. I love you now, God, and I
want to keep on loving you when
I'm grown up as well.

Dear God,
People can see what I'm doing.
People can hear what I'm saying.
But they don't know what I'm thinking.
You do.
You see what I'm doing, so help me to please you.
You hear what I'm saying, so help the words to be good.
You know what I'm thinking. Please stop all the nasty
thoughts from creeping in like worms. May my thoughts be
good to please you.

18

Thank you, God, that good mummies and other grown-ups look after their babies so well. They feed them and wash them and change their nappies and keep them safe and warm and love them. They know their names.

Thank you, God, that good shepherds look after their sheep so well. They take them into nice green fields to eat; they keep them safe and warm; they know each one by name.

Thank you, God, that you look after us so well. You have given us grown-ups to give us clothes and food. You know each of us by our names; and you love us very much. Thank you.

You know just what I'm thinking, Father. You know when I seem to boil up with hate inside me. You know when someone lets me down and I feel I could cry. You know when it isn't fair. Thank you that you understand all my thoughts. I'm sorry for the bad ones.
Thank you that you know all this about me and still love me.
Amen.

stories
about
God

I like stories, Jesus—stories about boys and girls; stories
of adventure; stories about ponies; about dolls; about
.... Thank you for the people who write the stories
and for those who draw the pictures.
Thank you for stories in the Bible, too. Sometimes they
are difficult to understand, but sometimes they are exciting.
I'm glad there are stories about you, Jesus, because that's
how we know what you're like. Please help me in my listening and in my reading. Amen.

We heard a story from the Bible today, God. It was about
.... We are so glad we have stories about you. I've
got a Bible story-book, with a .... cover. Some
people in other countries aren't allowed to read stories
from the Bible. We are glad we can. Thank you for telling
us about yourself. Help us to read the Bible more and more
as we get older. Amen.

special times to learn about God

A prayer for Saturday
God our Father, tomorrow we are going to Sunday School (Junior Church/Family Service) to worship you and to meet other boys, girls and grown-ups who want to worship you too. Help us as we get to know you better; as we learn new things about Jesus your Son; as we praise you and pray to you. Especially help our Sunday School teachers (Leaders/Clergy or Minister) as they decide all that we shall do with them tomorrow, and as they prepare the story they will tell us. We ask this so that we may all please Jesus. Amen.

Prayers for Sunday
Dear God, we have come to Sunday School (Junior Church/Family Service) today to think especially about you.
We want to tell you how wonderful you are.
We want to thank you for listening to our prayers.
We want to thank you for caring for us this past week.
Help us to praise you today.
Help us as we pray to you today.
Help us to learn about you today.
Help us to enjoy this time together. Amen.

For boys and girls who are not here

God in Heaven, not everyone is here today.

Some are not very well. Please help their Mummies and Daddies to look after them till they are fit again. Even when they feel hot and horrid, help them to remember that you love them.

Some boys and girls have gone out with their parents this week. Wherever they are now, help them to remember that you love them.

Some boys and girls we know, never come to Sunday School. Please help them to find out that you love them just as much as you love us. Amen.

Before the story

Dear Jesus, thank you that you are here with us this afternoon (morning).
Thank you for the Bible and all the stories written there.
Thank you that we can listen to one of those stories
   today.
Help us as we listen now.
Help us to learn about God, your Father.
Help us to learn about you and your love.
Amen.

Dear God, we are going home now. There'll be tea and perhaps the television and play and bed-time. Help us not to forget all about you when we've left Sunday School. Thank you that you don't just live in a church. You can be anywhere. Be with us when we eat and play. Make us nicer people because we love you. Amen.

talking to God

Thank you, Lord Jesus, that we can talk to you anywhere. We don't have to kneel down or be in a church or at Sunday School. Thank you that you are always listening and hear all we say. Amen.

Father, I sometimes wonder if you hear me when I pray, especially as millions of people must be talking to you at the same time. But I know you do listen and hear, because you haven't the same sort of mind or ears as a human being, but are much more special. Make me realise how wonderful and great you are, when I pray. Thank you that you are interested in little things as well as the big. Help me to tell you about everything. I want to know you better as a friend. I ask these things to please Jesus. Amen.

23

all the year round

Spring
Thank you, God, for spring-time.
The bare brown trees burst into blossom and green
   leaves.
Thank you, God, for spring-time.
The bulbs poke up their heads in their pots.
Thank you, God, for spring-time.
There are baby birds chirping and woolly lambs skipping.
Thank you, God, for spring-time.
It would be sad if the winter stayed all the year round.
I'm glad you thought of spring, God.
Thank you.

Spring is lovely, Lord. There are people out in their gardens talking to the people next door; there's more time to play outside after tea; there are wriggly tadpoles growing into frogs.
Spring is also special to you, Lord Jesus. You were killed and then you came alive again and talked to your friends. We remember all that at Easter. Make yourself alive and real to me all the time, please, Lord Jesus. I would like to have been one of your helpers and seen you properly, but I can still talk to you now, because you are alive.

25

Summer

I like summer, Lord Jesus.
I'm glad we can go to school without a thick winter coat.
I'm glad we can play out in the garden till it's bed-time.
I'm glad we have holidays and can go to the seaside or
  the country.
Thank you for giving us summer.

Autumn

Thank you, God, for the red and brown and coppery gold leaves that blow off the trees. Thank you for heaps of them, crackly and dry. We love to kick through them. Thank you that the trees haven't stopped growing. They are not dead. We know they'll have new green leaves next spring. We know this because you make them.

We thank you, dear God, that
    the little brown seed became
    the little green plant which had
    the pretty little flower that gave the fruit.
And now we have the fruit that you made. Thank you.
There are apples and pears cheap in the shops;
and blackberries along the prickly hedgerows.
There are squashy purple plums and gooseberries like
   green marbles.
Then there are oranges and bananas and peaches that
    come over the sea.
I'm glad you have made fruit for us, God.
Thank you.

Today we want to thank you specially, God, for our food. It's harvest-time, and we think of the people who have helped to grow it and get it for us.

Thank you for the farmer who cuts the yellow wheat for flour for our bread; thank you for the men who drive lorries of cabbages and carrots, lettuce and apples, from the farms to the shops.

Thank you for the men in the shops who sell us the brown potatoes and green pears and lots of other fruit and vegetables.

Thank you for the men who pilot ships which bring the oranges and bananas and grapes from other lands over the sea to the land where we live.

All these people help to bring us our food. Thank you for them. Amen.

27

Winter

There are special things to enjoy in winter, God.
Thank you for blankets of snow, marked by the footprints
  of birds.
Thank you for spiders' webs, sparkling with raindrops.
Thank you for slidy ice on the ponds.
Thank you for frost patterns in the windows.
You've made all these. Thank you.

Jesus, the snow is crunchy, outside. You probably never
saw it when you lived on earth, but you still know about it.
Thank you for the white carpet outside and the trees look-
ing so pretty. Help Daddy and those who drive on the
roads to be very careful. Amen.

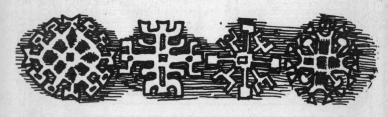

Dear Father, it's so cold outside. The roads were slippery
and I slithered to school; there are very few birds about
now, just the chirpy robin; and it gets dark almost before
tea.
It's winter.
I'm glad all the year doesn't feel the same.
I know that in this weather, lots of people will be
  miserable.
There are ragged children whose parents cannot afford to
  buy them clothes.
There are hungry children who have less to eat in a
  week than we do in a day.
Take care of them, please, Father. Make them look to you
in their unhappiness. Please comfort them, and help other
people to give more money and clothes and food to help
them. We ask this to please Jesus. Amen.

Lord Jesus, this morning I peeped out of the window and everything was white—sparkly white. Thank you. Thank you that we have warmth indoors—clothes to keep us warm when our breath steams out like a kettle; and food to keep us healthy. Help us to remember those who fear the cold weather because they don't have enough to wear or enough to eat. Amen.

things I like

Thank you for voices, Lord. It must be awful not being
   able to laugh or say 'Hello!'
I'm glad I can talk to my friends.
I'm glad I can whisper.
I'm glad I can sing, too.
Help me to say only nice things with my voice.
Help me to stop the nasty things from coming out.
May people know that I love you by what I say. Amen.

Dear Lord Jesus, I like *new*
things—new shoes, with a special
smell; new books of clear white
paper; new friends with secrets to
share. Thank you.

Thank you that we can feel things, Father.
—For the warm fur of dogs and cats;
—For the sand between our toes at the seaside;
—For the cold creamy feel of ice-cream in our mouths;
—For the thud of a football against our boots;
Thank you, heavenly Father.

I like the glistening raindrops, splashing on my
    window.
I like the fluffy snow-flakes dancing in the sky.
I like the gentle sunbeams, warm on my face.
God, you made all these, and I like you.

Dear God,
I love the crash of cymbals,
  and the squelch of my boots in the mud;
  and the ping of the door bell.
Thank you that I have ears to hear.
Thank you that you've made such different sounds. It would be awful to live in a silent world, like the television with the sound turned off. You have made the world just right. Thank you. Amen.

Dear God, thank you for colours
—for big red buses and yellow bull-dozers;
—for the grey motorway streaming through green
  countryside;
—for the pink on the tip of a daisy;
—for clear blue eyes.
I'm glad everything isn't just in grey and brown.
Thank you for colours. Amen.

Dear God, thank you for the television today. I watched
.... It was fun. Thank you for the clever people
who make the television work. Thank you for those who
write the stories for it. May they do the best they can so
that the programmes please you, Lord Jesus, and don't
make you sad. Amen.

Thank you for the *television*, God. It's amazing that we can
see exactly what's happening at the other side of the world,
just by sitting down in our homes and watching this little
box.
The men who invented it must have been ever so clever.
Thank you for the *telephone*, God. It's fun to talk to Auntie
.... or Granny or .... down a little wire.
There must be wires criss-crossing all over the country
and under the sea.
The men who invented telephones must have been ever
  so clever.
Thank you for the *record player*, God. Records are like
talking books. My favourite is ....
The men who invented them must have been ever so
  clever.
God, you must be much more clever than these inventors.
You can see each of us without television and we can talk
to you without a telephone.
Thank you, God, that you thought of everything.

Dear God, I love to see the tiny fish in the tank. They make bubbles and swim up and down. I like to feel the smooth fur of the cat as she rubs against my legs. I like to see the dog's wet tongue and wagging tail as he rushes at me to say 'Hello!' I love to watch the hamster and the budgie in their cages.

Thank you so much for pets. Help me to look after my .... well and be kind to him/her.

Dear God, I'm glad lots of animals are friendly and that we can have them as pets.

Thank you for the snowy-white baby rabbits all warm and cosy in a heap together;

Thank you for purring cats with silky fur and eyes like marbles;

Thank you for the little brown hamster treading round his wheel;

Thank you for blue and yellow budgies cheeping happily in their cages;

Thank you for dogs—ginger ones with floppy ears; little ones who get very excited; friendly ones who rush at you.

God, my pet is a ....

Help me to be very kind, always remembering to feed him/her and to clean out his/her home.

If I forget, he/she can't say anything to remind me.

Help me to show special love to ....

Lord Jesus, I'm learning to play the .... and it's not easy. Help me to stick at the dull exercises. I want to enjoy gay tunes later on and make real music. Music is lovely, Lord. We can sing to it, dance to it, or just listen. Thank you, Lord. Amen.

Noises are fun.

I like splashing in the bath, and the tick of Daddy's watch.

I like the purring of the cat, and the front door bell.

Dear God, help me to be quiet when shouting would make people cross.

Help me to be gentle when banging about would annoy people. Amen.

Dear God, we're glad we can jump and skip and run. Some boys and girls can't because they are ill and have something wrong with their legs. Help them to have fun in other ways. Amen.

Games are fun, Lord Jesus. When you were a boy, you must have enjoyed them. I like dashing down the field and kicking the ball. It's exciting to score a goal. Help me always to play fairly, and not to foul. Help me to do the best I can in playing games, because I want to please you. Amen.

Thank you for the games we play, Lord Jesus. It's fun pretending to be space-men, or princesses, or pop-stars; it's fun jumping and skipping and running after each other; it's fun playing around with a ball.

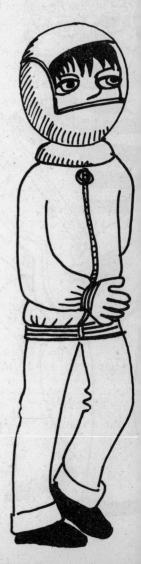

The slides in the park are fun, Lord. Whooooooooosh! I slip to the bottom. The swings in the park are fun, Lord, up and up I go. The things to climb are fun, too. I climb over and round and in and out. Thank you for fun in the park. Amen.

Thank you, God, for stories. Some are exciting, some are fun, some take us into a different world. Thank you for people who write books. Thank you for shops and libraries where we can get them.

Lord Jesus, I'm learning to read and I've got as far as .... in my reading book. I like words.
I like big words like 'umbrella' and little words like 'if'.
Soon I'll be able to read stories about you.
Sometime I'll be able to read out of the Bible.
Thank you for books.
Thank you for your special book, the Bible. Amen.

special times

Birthdays
Lord Jesus, it's my birthday today. I am .... years old. I love everything special about today—my presents— I've had .... and ....
—the cake with candles on it.
I don't want to forget about you, today. And while I am .... I want to please you in everything I do, and not make you sad. I want this next year to be even better than the last. I can only do this with your help. Amen.

New Year

God, there's a big new year to come, and it's like an
empty page.
I don't want it to be full of blots, and messy things.
I want it to be kept neat and beautiful for you.
So please stop me from being selfish and wanting my own
way.
Please stop me from being unkind, and making other
people cry.
Please stop me from saying 'I won't,' and not doing as
Mummy and Daddy say.
Help me to be kind, and loving, all through this year.
Amen.

Sundays

Sundays are different, Lord. Make us very helpful at home
and happy to do things together as a family. Help us to
remember that you came alive again on a Sunday, and that
you are still alive today.

Help me specially to remember you, today, Lord Jesus,
even if those around me don't love you. Thank you that
you are always with me on each day of the week.

Dear God, we want this day to be special for you. Thank
you that we are all at home together and can talk and play
and eat as a family. When we go to church to worship you,
help us to mean what we say and sing, because we do love
you. May Jesus have an important part in today.

The Zoo
I've just been to the Zoo, God.
I've seen the great big
   elephants.
You made them enormous.
I've seen the tall giraffes.
You made their very long necks.
I've seen the prickly porcupines.
You made them spiky, too.
I'm glad animals are all different.
Help the keepers to look after
   them kindly, please God.

We went to the Zoo today (this week), God. There were so many different animals. We laughed at the monkeys swinging above. We kept away from the roaring lions, and held our hands over our ears in the noisy bird-house. I specially liked the .... You thought up lots and lots of different animals, God. They came from Australia and Africa and India and all sorts of places. Thank you that you didn't make animals the same all over the world.

Seaside Holidays

Jesus, you were often at the sea-side, talking to fishermen, going out in boats. Thank you that we are having a holiday by the sea. We don't know if it's going to rain all the time or be sunny and hot. Help us to enjoy the holiday whatever the weather, and not to grumble if it's wet.

Lord Jesus, it's ever such fun by the sea-side. I like it on the beach with the sand trickling through my toes and the waves rushing in. I like Mummy and Daddy being there to play with. Thank you that you made the little specks of sand and the great big sea. Thank you, too, for Mummy and Daddy. Amen.

43

Safety

Tomorrow we're going on a journey to .... Please keep us safe as we travel. Help the drivers to be careful and kind. Help us not to make too much noise if we're excited, or to grumble if we get bored. Thank you that you can be with us wherever we go. We just can't hide from your love.

In Jesus' name. Amen.

Dear God, we know people have to be very careful if they're to be safe on the roads. We pray for all those who drive to work. Keep them patient and willing to give way to others. We pray for all those who drive vans and lorries and buses about all day. Keep them on the look-out for dangers. We pray for all the people walking on the roads, and those cycling. Make them think before they cross roads, and really watch what they are doing. Amen.

44

I like riding on top of big shiny buses.
  Please keep them safe on the roads, God.
I like speeding through fields and towns in fast trains.
  Please keep them safe on their tracks, God.
I like being driven in Daddy's comfy car.
  Please keep it safe wherever it goes, God.
Thank you. Amen.

my home

Lord Jesus, you were brought up in a home in Nazareth, with Mary and Joseph and your brothers. Thank you that you've put me in a family. We quarrel sometimes, and I know we shouldn't, but thank you that most of the time we feel close to each other. Amen.

Dear God,
I'm glad you know all about us in our family—Mum, Dad, ... and .... and me. We all come in at different times, and we all like doing different things. We're sorry, God, when we squabble over who's having what on the tele. We're sorry, God, when we answer back and fight. We're sorry, God, when we want our own ways. May our home be a place where Jesus is loved.

Dear God, today we want to say thank you for our mothers and those who care for us at home. If we were left without them, who would cook our meals or mend our clothes? Who would we tell about everything that had happened at school? Who would there be to turn to, when we were miserable?
Thank you for the love they show us. Thank you for the way they work hard for us. Forgive us for the times when we have grumbled, or upset them. Help us to show our love to them in many helpful ways. Amen.

Dear God, Dad goes out to .... Mum works at .... Please help them to do their best for you each day. Keep us from being so full of ourselves that we don't think of helping them. Amen.

Dear God, in my family there is
Mummy and Daddy and ....
We have lots of fun together.
Thank you that there's another
family—of all the boys and girls
and men and women who believe
in you. Amen.

Lord Jesus, Thank you for my
family. Thank you for Mummy
and Daddy and ....
Thank you for the good times we
have together:
—For the games we play;
   (Help me not to mind about
   losing.)
—For the places we go to;
   (Make me interested in
   everything around me.)
—For the meals we have
   together (I like .... and
   .... best.)
Jesus, you grew up as a boy in a
family. You must have been good
fun to have around. Help me to
think of others first—and to be
really helpful in the home. I
know I can only do this with your
help.
I ask for it, to please you. Amen.

Dear God, I'm missing Mummy
(Daddy*) a lot. I wish she was
back with us. It's not the same at
home. Help me to be brave. I
know she'd like me to be cheerful
and not to mope. Show me how I
can help her best when she comes
back. Amen.
* If it's Daddy, watch in this
prayer for other words that you
will need to change, too.

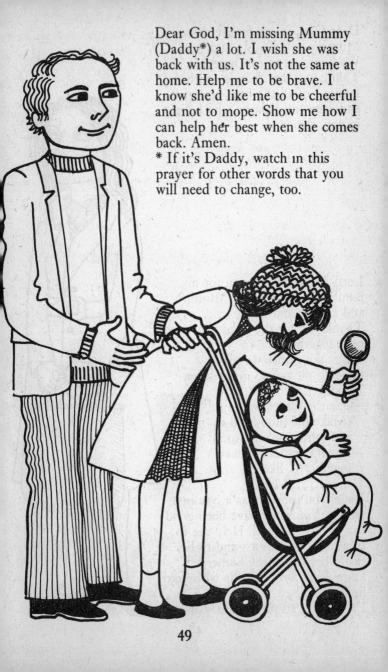

49

Thank you for sisters and brothers and cousins and friends, Lord Jesus. We would be very lonely without them. Help us to share our toys and sweets. Help us to be kind. You lived on earth in a family, and you had brothers and friends as well. You were always kind, gentle and fun to play with. Help us to be like you were. Amen.

Just before I go to sleep, I want to talk to you, Jesus.
I'm sorry for .... today.
I know you were sad about that. Thank you that you
    have forgiven me.
We had a lovely time today ....
I know you were pleased about it. Thank you for fun
    and laughter.
Jesus, I'm glad you are with me all through the night.
    Give me a good sleep.
Good-night, Jesus.

things
to
eat

For good food, Father, we thank
  you:
—for chocolate cake
—for butter oozing into toast
—for popping cereals
—for chips wrapped up
—for ice-cream and custard
—for sausages sizzling together in
  the pan.
Thank you for these. Some people
don't know if they'll have any
breakfast when they get up in the
morning. Make us very grateful
for what we have. Amen.

Dear God, you are a kind Father
who always knows what we need.
Thank you very much for this
lovely food. Amen.

Dear Father in heaven, there is lots of good food just waiting to be eaten. Thank you for .... —who got it ready. Thank you, too, for the food. Amen.

Thank you for all your presents to us, dear God. We have friends, and our family, and a home, and plenty of food to eat. Thank you now for this meal we are going to eat. Amen.

Dear God, thank you for breakfast. For crunchy flakes (or ....) and toast and milk, thank you. It's school today and I'll see .... and .... and .... again. They've had breakfast too. Thank you for giving us good food to eat. We ask you to help those who are so poor that they have to go to school without any breakfast. Amen.

Dear Lord Jesus, that was a lovely meal. Thank you. I specially liked the .... and the .... We need to eat to keep us alive, but thank you that it is also something nice to do. Help us to remember that there are boys and girls in different parts of the world who are always hungry. They never have enough. They would snap up the bits we leave. So stop us from being greedy. Amen.

at school

Lord Jesus, I'm going back to school today (tomorrow, this week). I'm sorry for the times I didn't do my best or didn't do what I was told. Thank you that you have forgiven and forgotten already. Please give me the help of the Holy Spirit during this new term (year). Help me to get on with people better—even those in the class who don't like me. Help me to do what the teacher tells me—even when I don't want to. Help me to work hard and do my best for you. Amen.

Lord Jesus, we want today to be a *good* day at school. Please keep us from squabbling and cheating. Help us to be kind and helpful. Help us to do what we're told, quickly. We know that the things we do will be much more fun that way. Amen.

Dear God, at the beginning of this day at school, we want to think of you and say how much we love you. You see each one of us when we draw in our books, or add up sums. You can recognize each one of us when we play skipping or ball or tag in the playground. Help us to please you all through this day by being helpful to each other and the teachers. Amen.

Dear God, we want to think about you at the beginning of this day at school. You have made us.
You have given us minds to work out sums.
You have given us hands to paint pictures with.
You have given us eyes to see colours and shapes.
You have given us ears to hear music.
May our minds, hands, eyes and ears please you today.
Stop us from doing anything that would make you sad.
Amen.

Dear God, sometimes at school
the others do much better than I
do. They learn to read faster and
add up sums right. Help me
always to do my best, not just to
please my teacher, but to please
you.

Father, you know I'm not very clever at some lessons, even when I try hard. Help me not to mind when other boys and girls tease me, but to keep doing my best, for your sake. In Jesus' name. Amen.

Dear Lord Jesus, sometimes I'm left out at school, or I haven't got a special friend, like everyone else. I feel it's unfair, but please show me if there is something about me that's not very nice, so that I can do something about it. Also, please keep me from being hurt and curling up into a ball like a hedgehog with my prickles. Thank you that you know all about me and want the best for me.

Jesus, it isn't fair at school. People sometimes tell tales about me. Sometimes they won't talk, and sometimes they won't play. Help me not to mind too much. When I think I haven't got a friend, may I remember that you can be my friend. Amen.

Dear, God, we learnt in school
today about .... It's
quite fun, the way our teacher
tells it. Thank you for our school
and for the teachers.

We pray for boys and girls who
live in this country, but come
from other countries. It must feel
strange for them. Help us not to
make it more difficult for them at
school, but to be just as friendly
to them as to everyone else.

57

**people
who
help**

There are so many people we see around us, God.
There's the person at the cash-desk in the supermarket.
Please help her to smile and be patient with everyone.
There's the lady (man) who helps us cross the road. Keep
her warm enough as she waits there.
There's the man who drives the bus. Help him to drive
safely.
There's the postman with his letters. Help him not to mind
the weather.
There's the milkman clanking down the bottles. Please
keep him cheerful.
There's the policeman, and the teacher, and the dustbin
man and so many more.
Thank you, God, that there are so many people to help us.
Amen.

Dear God, thank you that the dentist is so clever with his
little mirror and shiny tools. Thank you that he's there to
help our teeth stay as good as they can be. When he has to
hurt a little, help us to be brave. We are glad he looks after
our teeth. Amen.

Dear God, our doctor has to see so many people every day.
Some have coughs and some colds and some are very ill.
He helps each one to get better.
Please keep him well.
Please make him kind.
Please keep him going when he's tired.
Thank you for him. Amen.

God, there are so many people
helping us. There's the policeman,
telling the traffic when to go;
there's the milkman clanking
down the bottles each
morning; there's the bus
conductor taking our money on
the bus. Thank you that they do
their work so well. Make them
kind all through the day even
when they're tired. Amen.

friends

Jesus, you had some friends—Peter and John. Thank you for my friends, for .... and .... Thank you that we can play together and be together at school. Jesus, you never left anyone out all lonely. Help me to be loving like you. Help me to be friends with the boy or girl who is lonely. Amen.

Dear Lord Jesus, I don't like .... very much. Help me to think of the best things about her (him) and not to think about the way she's (he's) not nice. You love her (him) a lot, just the same as you love me. Amen.

Dear God, my friends are all so different from each other.
One is tall, and one is fat.
One has curly hair and one has straight hair.
One has blue eyes and one has brown eyes.
I am ....
I have .... hair.
I have .... eyes.
Thank you that you've made each one of us different.
  Amen.

I don't think I want to grow old, Lord.
I couldn't skip and jump, and my skin would go all wrinkly,
and I couldn't play with trains or dolls on the floor.
But you have made people like that, Lord Jesus. They all
grow from babies to boys and girls to grown-ups to old
people. So it must be good.
Help me to *help* them
  —not shout or bang doors nearby;
  —not pretend they aren't there;
Jesus, if you were here, you would have been very kind.
Help me to please you when I meet .... or
....